How to Pack an Alpaca Pack

written by: Cowboy Worm

illustrated by: Jacquelyn Young
Nathan Young
and Johnny Worm

published by:

Stone Brook Publishers

Attica , Indiana

edited by:

Johnny Worm

to Jyn

Grandpa's little inspiration

For the Reader

When you read to a his/her,

Choose the gender of each alpaca in your story

All girls

All boys

or some of each

My hope is that this book will educate and introduce many to this noble creature, the alpaca.

Alpacas come from places in the Andes,

Like Chile and Peru

And they are very kind to me, and to you.

If you need more, let's say Equador.

An alpaca's eye is round and big in size,

Alpaca coats come in light; fawn, white, silver, or gray.

Or dark; red, brown,
coffee, black, and bay.
And sometimes dark gray.

Alpacas have ears that point to the sky

Easier to hear both you and I.

You might hear mmmm, with an alpaca near. Is that an alpaca hum that I hear?

They have feet with two toes that grip stone or dirt, so they don't fall down, and get hurt.

An alpaca can carry a pack, both high and low,

Now to pack an alpaca pack,

you need a saddle for an alpaca back.

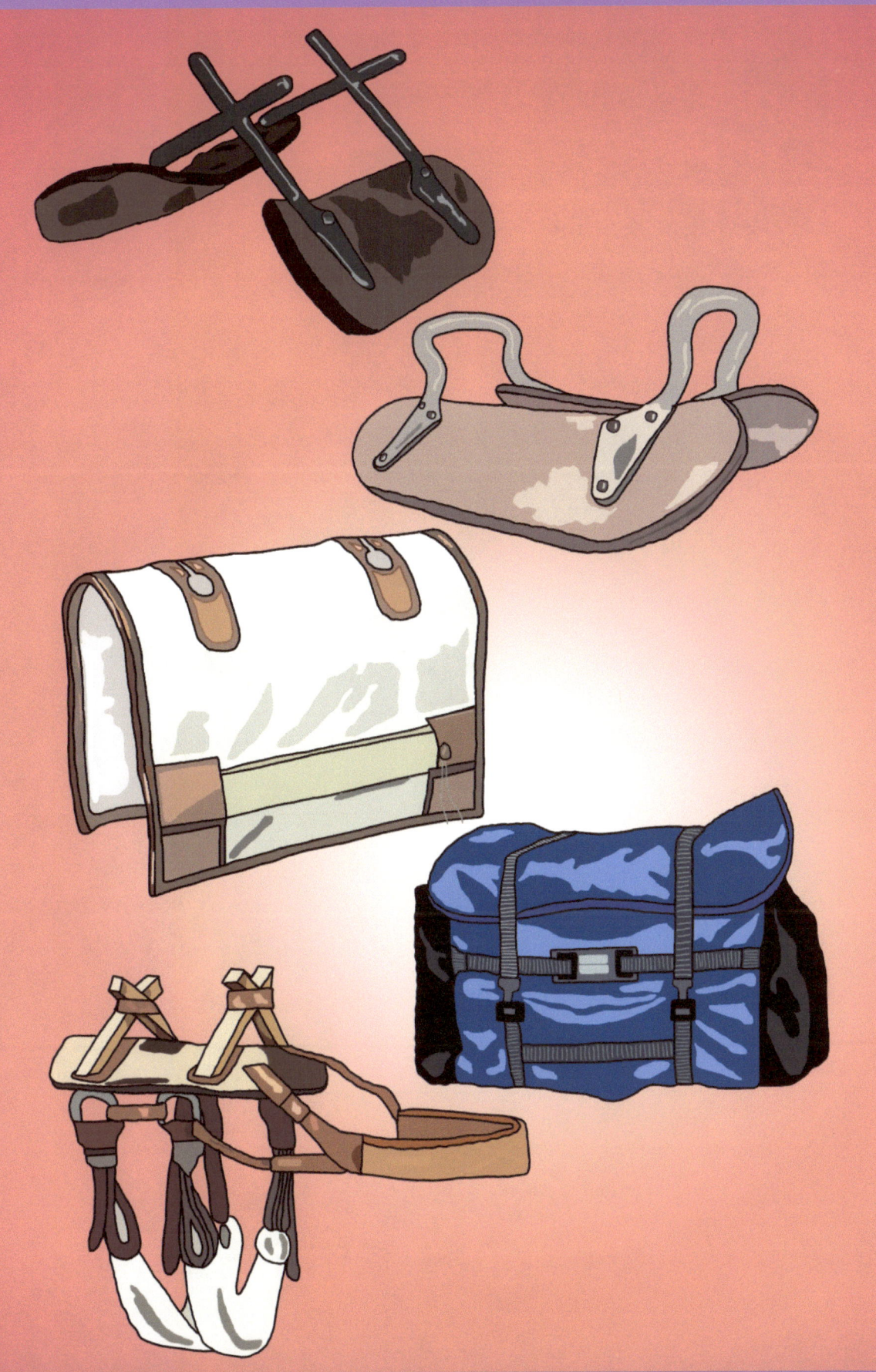

You wouldn't want to pack an alpaca pack,

that word, would be an alpaca herd.

To pack an alpaca pack,

on the top

of an alpaca back,

it's a cinch,

to cinch it up right,

just center it

and pull it up tight.

Now it won't slip or slide,

and the alpaca,

won't fall on his/her side.

Once it's full and tied up tight, you know you have packed the alpaca pack right.

Now take the rope that is tied neatly on the alpaca's face,

and you can lead him/her anyplace.

What a wonderful end to a beautiful day

**Will you be my friend?
How about some hay?**

Cover - Blue Sky Curious Alpaca picture
by: Pat Gaines

Page 3 - 3 alpacas lying down picture from
Sunset Accoyo sales@accoyo.org

Page 8 - A pair of young alpacas at the pre-Inca burial site of Sillustani, Peru CCASA 2.5 generic license
by: Christophe Meneboeuf

Page 9 - Vicugna pacos CCASA 2.0 generic license by: Kyle Flood from Victoria, British Columbia, Canada

Page 12, 13 - a picture of alpacas in Equador (wikipedia.org) by: Philippe Lavoie

Page 16 - Large alpaca with the body covered with soft woolly curls CCASA 4.0 International license by: Federico Candoni notes added, no other alterations

Page 17 - Alpaca, CCASA 2.0 generic license
by: Eva Rinaldi, Sydney Austrailia

Page 18 - Alpaca in Cusco Region, Peru CCASA 4.0 International license by: Alexey Komarov

Page 23 - Peruvian baby alpaca picture from Fells Andes webpage, derived from mallkini.com.pe/farm

Page 30 - An Alpaca (Vicugna Pacos) in the snow at the Cincinnati Zoo CCA 2.0 generic license Flickr Alpaca
by: Mark Dumont (hay enhanced)

Back cover - Sunshine on Alpaca herd by: Sol Alpaca
www.solalpaca.com

Creative Commons Attribution Share Alike-CCASA

A large thank you to the Alpaca Community, your contribution big or small, is appreciated one and all.

www.ingramcontent.com/pod-product-compliance
Lightning Source LLC
Chambersburg PA
CBHW041156290426
44108CB00002B/85